Y0-EGG-575

THE CHRISTMAS STORY AS TOLD
IN THE GOSPELS

ABINGDON PRESS
Nashville

IN THE BEGINNING was the Word, and the Word was with God, and the Word was God. He was with God in the beginning.

Through him all things were made; without him nothing was made that has been made. In him was life, and that life

was the light ... The light shines in the darkness, but the darkness has not understood it. He was in the world, and though the world was made through him, the world did not recognize him.

JOHN 1:1-5, 10

IN THE TIME OF Herod king of Judea there was a priest named Zechariah. His wife was Elizabeth. They had no children.

An angel of the Lord appeared to Zechariah. He was startled and gripped with fear. But the angel said to him: "Do not be afraid, Zechariah; your prayer has been heard. Your wife Elizabeth will bear you a son, and you are to give him the name John."

Zechariah asked the angel, "How can I be sure of this? I am an old man and my wife is well on in years."

The angel answered, "I am Gabriel. I have been sent to tell you this good news. And now you will not be able to speak until the day this happens."

LUKE 1:5, 7, 11–13, 18

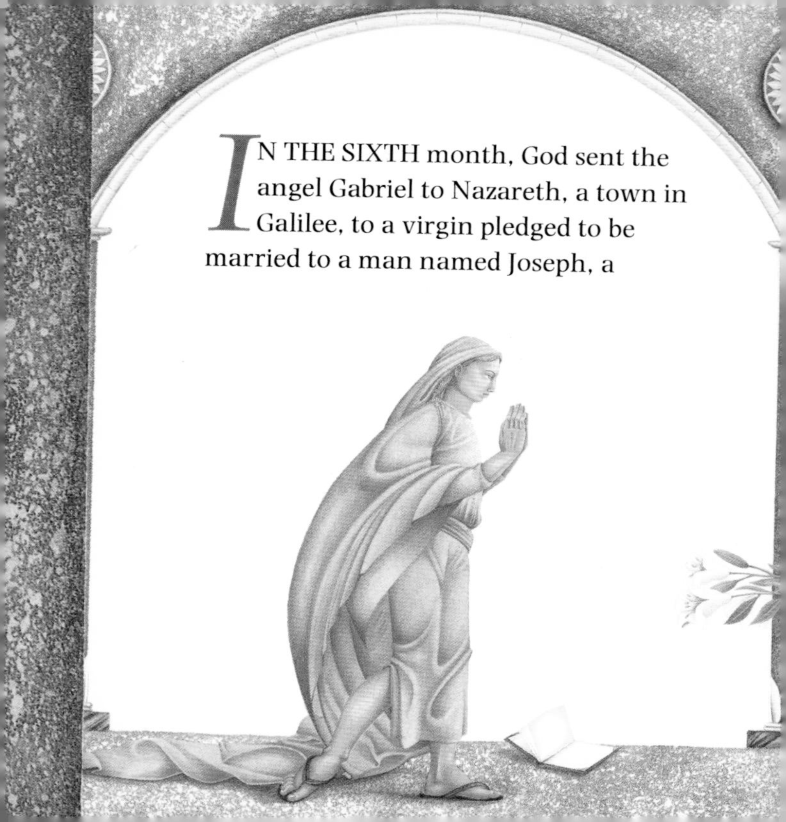

IN THE SIXTH month, God sent the angel Gabriel to Nazareth, a town in Galilee, to a virgin pledged to be married to a man named Joseph, a descendant of David. The virgin's name was Mary. The angel went to her and said, "Greetings, you who are highly favored! The Lord is with you. You will give birth to a son, and you are to give him the name Jesus."

LUKE 1:26-28, 31

AT THAT TIME Mary got ready and hurried to a town in the hill country of Judea, where she entered Zechariah's home and greeted Elizabeth. When Elizabeth heard Mary's greeting, the baby leaped in her womb, and Elizabeth was filled with the Holy Spirit.

In a loud voice she exclaimed: "Blessed are you among women, and blessed is the child you will bear! But why am I so favored, that the mother of my Lord should come to me? As soon as the sound of your greeting reached my ears, the baby in my womb leaped for joy. Blessed is she who has believed that what the Lord has said to her will be accomplished!"

LUKE 1:39-45

WHEN IT WAS TIME for Elizabeth to have her baby, she gave birth to a son. On the eighth day they came to circumcise the child, and they were going to name him after his father Zechariah, but his mother spoke up and said, "No! He is to

be called John." They made signs to his father, to find out what he would like to name the child. He asked for a writing tablet, and he wrote, "His name is John." Immediately Zechariah began to speak, praising God.

LUKE 1:57, 59–64

THIS IS HOW THE birth of Jesus Christ came about: His mother Mary was pledged to be married to Joseph, but before they came together, she was found to be with child through the Holy Spirit. Because Joseph was a righteous man and did not want to expose her to public disgrace, he had in mind to divorce her quietly.

But an angel of the Lord appeared and said, "Joseph, do not be afraid to take Mary home as your wife, because what is conceived in her is from the Holy Spirit. She will give birth to a son, and you are to give him the name Jesus, because he will save his people from their sins."

MATTHEW 1:18–21

IN THOSE DAYS Caesar Augustus issued a decree that a census should be taken of the entire Roman world. So Joseph went up from Nazareth to Bethlehem. While they were there, the time came for the baby to be born, and she gave birth to her firstborn, a son. She wrapped him in cloths and placed him in a manger, because there was no room for them in the inn.

And there were shepherds living out in the fields near by, keeping watch over their flocks at night. Suddenly a great company of the heavenly host appeared praising God and saying, "Glory to God in the highest, and on earth, peace."

LUKE 2:1–8, 13–14

ON THE EIGHTH day, when it was time to circumcise him, he was named Jesus, the name the angel had given him. Joseph and Mary took Jesus to Jerusalem to present him to the Lord. Now there was a man in Jerusalem called Simeon, who was righteous and devout. Moved by the Spirit, he went into the temple courts. When the parents brought in the child Jesus, Simeon took him in his arms and praised God, saying: "Sovereign Lord, as you have promised, you now dismiss your servant in peace. For my eyes have seen your salvation, which you have prepared in the sight of all people."

LUKE 2:21–22, 25, 27–31

AFTER JESUS WAS born in Bethlehem in Judea, during the time of King Herod, Magi (Wise Men) from the east came to Jerusalem and asked, "Where is the one who has been born king of the Jews? We saw his star in the east and have come to worship him." King Herod called the Magi secretly and found out from them the exact time

the star had appeared. They went on their way, and the star went ahead of them until it stopped over the place where the child was. Coming to the house they opened their treasures and presented Jesus with gifts of gold and incense and myrrh.

MATTHEW 2:1-2, 7, 9, 11

WHEN THE Magi had gone, an angel of the Lord appeared to Joseph in a dream. "Get up," he said, "take the child and his mother and escape to Egypt. Stay there until I tell you, for Herod is going to search for the child to kill him."

So he got up, took the child and his

mother during the night and left for Egypt, where he stayed until the death of Herod.

When Herod realized that he had been outwitted by the Magi, he was furious, and he gave orders to kill all the boys in Bethlehem who were two years old and under.

MATTHEW 2:13–14, 16

AFTER HEROD DIED, an angel of the Lord appeared in a dream to Joseph in Egypt and said, "Get up, take the child and his mother and go to the land of Israel, for those who were trying to take the child's life are dead."

So he got up, took the child and his mother and went and lived in a town called Nazareth.

MATTHEW
2:19–21, 23